AYE, NO!

a full-length play

Liz Coronado Castillo

ISBN-979-8-218-12671-1

Cover design by: Johnny Rodriguez
Library of Congress Control Number: 2022924079
Printed in the United States of America
For production rights contact Liz Coronado Castillo castliz32@gmail.com

Thank you to my playwriting professor, Dr. Norman Bert, for your guidance and wisdom. Thank you to all the artists who gave their time and talent during the workshopping process.

Original One-Act; Texas Tech University:

CAST
Ana: Cassandra Gallegos
Francisca: Holly Garza
Mague: Nadia Bodie
Maria: Claudia Acosta
Joe: Gabriel Vasquez
Cathy: Karen Moore
Crystal: Brice Russell

PRODUCTION STAFF
Director: Justin Cypert
Stage Manager: Stephanie Berry
Dramaturg: Mary Housewirth
Costume Designer: Sarah Bray
Light/Sound Designer: Chris Leffel
Scenic Designer: Zachary Elms

Original Full-Length; Sul Ross State University

CAST
Kika: Brenda Gallegos
Mague: Sylvia Samayoa
Maria: Anya Reyes/Elizabeth Gutierrez
Alicia: Chrisanta
Cathy: Carrie Turney
Zereda: David DeLaO
Starlinda: Miguel Pena
Starkisha: Andrew Ross
Joe: Cory Hill/Calvin Landrum
Jehovah's Witness/Understudy: Derek Rhein

PRODUCTION STAFF
Director: Dona W. Roman
Technical Director: Jay Sawyer
Stage Manager: Joseph Rosco
Set Design: Jay Sawyer
Costume and Sound Design: Dona W. Roman
Light Design: Russell Calder
Set Construction: Joseph Rosco, Mark Sexton, Cory Hill, Derek Rhein
Costume Construction: Jenny Tavarez, Marisela Baca, Brenda Gallegos, Olivia Gallegos, Missy Wallace
Graphic Design: Lauren Mendias

CAST OF CHARACTERS

<u>ALICIA</u> - A college student.

<u>KIKA</u> - Alicia's grandmother.

<u>MAGUE</u> - KIKA's sister-in-law.

<u>MARIA</u> - KIKA's sister.

<u>JOE</u> - A college student.

<u>CATHY</u> - A college student.

<u>ZEREDA</u> - A Chicana drag queen.

<u>STARKISHA</u> - A Black drag queen.

<u>STARLINDA</u> - A Chicana drag queen.

<u>THE TIME</u>
The present.

<u>THE PLACE</u>
A border town on the US/Mexico border.

SCENES

ACT I

ACT II

ACT ONE

SCENE ONE

SETTING: A stage. The curtain is closed.

AT RISE: As the house music fades down ZEREDA comes out from behind the curtain in the center.

ZEREDA: Well hello everyone. Welcome, welcome. It's good to see all you beautiful people out here tonight...the rest of you too. Where's the Raza at? I haven't seen this many highlights since my cousin Rosie took half a year of cosmetology...or as she called it, cosmetelogical sciences. I'd like to tell you a little story tonight. Once upon a time there was a little girl who dreamt of falling in love. No, wait, that's not the right one...once upon a time there was a Mexican little girl who dreamt of falling in love. No...I have to get this just right...once upon a time there was a gay little Mexican girl raised by her *wela* and two nosey aunts. This was a little girl who thought her dreams were like everyone else's.

(The curtain opens.)

END OF SCENE

SCENE TWO

SETTING: KIKA's kitchen.

AT RISE: The curtains open to reveal KIKA and MAGUE sitting at a table drinking coffee and cleaning beans.

KIKA: What do you think about these kids today? What do they think life is?

MAGUE: They are so lazy and *delicados*. *Pues que*, we can't eat this and we can't eat that. When we were young it was good just to have something to eat.

KIKA: Yes, and, we can't eat beans cause they'll make us fart. I say fart. *Sabes que una vez* I heard that someone died because they held in a fart too long.

MAGUE: Oh, *si*. I remember. It happened to that boy that lived in that ranch next to us.

KIKA: *Si*. It was *Chilo's* son. He was at a dance talking to a girl and he was embarrassed to fart so he held it in.

MAGUE: *Pobre muchacho*.

KIKA: May he rest in peace.

   (They both do the sign of the cross.)

MAGUE: Que bonitos estan estos frijoles.

KIKA: *Los compre en el* Safe Way.

MAGUE: *Y María?*

KIKA: *Ya le llame.* The coffee's ready. She said she was dying her hair.

MAGUE: It's going to turn green again.

KIKA: Tell her something.

MAGUE: She's your sister.

KIKA: You're in the family too.

MAGUE: *Ay,* last month she walked in to church with her hair bright maroon.

KIKA: And then she sits right in the front.

MAGUE: Right next to *La Señora Isela. Mujer cochina* going around with all those *viejos.*

KIKA: Dicen que anda con el Flaco.

MAGUE: *Pero si el Flaco anda con la* Nancy.

KIKA: *Huy, eso no le importa a la Isela.*

MAGUE: Did you tell Maria that Alicia was coming today?

KIKA: *Pues, si.*

MAGUE: *Como tarda en llegar.* Is she still bringing a friend?

KIKA: Yes! I think she is finally getting married.

MAGUE: I was getting a little worried. I thought maybe she wasn't going to catch herself a nice good boy. I hope it's someone like my *Jesus.*

KIKA: *No! Por Dios no.* He's lazy.

MAGUE: What!

KIKA: Tu sabes que es verdad.

MAGUE: No...

KIKA: *Cuando andábamos en la limpia era muy flojo*; always wanted to stay at home and watch the TV.

MAGUE: He was nine.

KIKA: That don't matter.

MAGUE: See how you are.

KIKA: Nomas que sea Mexicano.

MAGUE: Y si se te apronta con un gringito?

KIKA: Aye no. Ni lo digas.

   (MARIA enters.)

MARIA: *Buenos días.* Is she here yet?

KIKA: Not yet.

MARIA: Did you hear about Marisol?

MAGUE: *No, que?*

MARIA: *Pues,* you know I don't like to spread rumors because *a Jesus no le gusta* but, they say that her husband introduced her to a young man because he has a bad heart and wants her to be happy.

MAGUE: No?

KIKA: *Pues,* at least he's thinking of her needs.

MAGUE: *No lo creo.*

MARIA: *Pues es lo que dicen.*

MAGUE: And she sits in the front too.

MARIA: I can't wait to meet *Alicia's* fiancé. I prayed my rosary first thing this morning so that everything goes good.

MAGUE: That's nice.

MARIA: I hope he's just like my *Jr.*

MAGUE: *Ay no.*

MARIA: Why not?

MAGUE: Cause he's lazy.

MARIA: No, he's just had some bad luck with jobs.

MAGUE: Remember when he didn't want to work in the fields.

MARIA: He was too little.

KIKA: I remember.

MAGUE: That's no excuse.

MARIA: *Bueno*, I'm just happy that she finally found someone. I was getting worried. Girls her age should either be married or be nuns and its clear she isn't going to be a nun...

MAGUE: Let's just hope he's nice...and Mexican.

KIKA: *Si*. That way I don't have to worry anymore about someone taking care of her if something happens to me.

MARIA: We'll take care of her if you die.

KIKA: What makes you think that I'm going to die before you?

MAGUE: We are younger.

KIKA: You can't tell. Like I was saying, I have been praying to *La Virgen de San Juan* for three months now and it worked. And I went to see *Juana* and asked for help.

MAGUE: She's a good *curandera*. She has a real gift.

MARIA: Uh-huh. She cured my JR from the drinking. Did you know that she is not going to do it anymore?

KIKA: *Válgame. Y yo que necesito una limpia.* I've been feeling like something is wrong.

MARIA: You're not going to let them sleep in the same room are you?

KIKA: No! Como se te ocurre eso?

MARIA: Do you know anything about him?

KIKA: Nada.

MARIA: What if he's black?

KIKA: *Ay no.*

MAGUE: I bet he's white!

KIKA: *Ya no digan tonterías!* Look at us; judging him before we even meet him.

> (ALICIA enters.)

ALICIA: I'm home!

> (All three LADIES get up and hug her and ad-lib their greetings.)

It's good to see you too.

MAGUE: And your boyfriend?

ALICIA: I have missed you.

MARIA: Where is he?

KIKA: You said that you were bringing a friend home.

ALICIA: I didn't say boyfriend...

KIKA: And you said you had something really important to tell us.

MAGUE: We thought that maybe you fell in love while you were at college.

ALICIA: How are you guys? How's everyone?

KIKA: Que tienes...

ALICIA: Nothing. I'm doing good in school and...and well, I did meet someone.

(The LADIES cheer and hug each other.)

KIKA: I told you. Ay, thank you *Virgen de San Juan*.

ALICIA: Sit down.

MARIA: Oh no.

ALICIA: No, there's no "oh no"...I just mean lets all sit down.

KIKA: Are you hungry? Do you want something to eat?

MAGUE: You look a little *flaca*.

MARIA: Are you on drugs?

KIKA: Drogas!

MARIA: I knew it! I saw something on *Primer Impacto*...

ALICIA: No! I'm just working out and eating right.

MARIA: You go off to college and all of a sudden our food isn't good enough?

KIKA: *Pues, come caca* then.

ALICIA: I didn't say that. I'm just tired of being chubby.

MAGUE: Chubby? *Hija*, you were fat.

MARIA: Uh-huh. But its not all your fault cause a large percentage of Americans are fat. I read about it online.

MAGUE: *Mira, mira la* know-it-all Miss America.

MARIA: Who doesn't know that?

KIKA/ MAGUE: We don't.

ALICIA: Hello…

KIKA: Don't interrupt.

ALICIA: Can I bring in my friend?

KIKA: Yes! Go get him!

(ALICIA exits.)

Be nice to him we don't want to scare him off.

MARIA: What are you saying?

KIKA: Nothing. I'm just saying.

MAGUE: What are you just saying?

KIKA: Nothing.

(ALICIA enters with CATHY.)

ALICIA: I want you to meet Cathy.

KIKA: Oh, he brought someone to speak for him.

MAGUE: Oh *si, muy* traditional. She must be the sister.

ALICIA: No, I just brought Cathy.

MARIA: *No que* she was bringing a boyfriend.

MAGUE: You dyed your hair for nothing.

KIKA: What happened to your boyfriend?

(MARIA does the sign of the cross.)

ALICIA: I don't have a boyfriend...

KIKA: Como que no!

ALICIA: *Ama*...I'm not sure how to say this...

MARIA: Then don't say it.

ALICIA: Tia, please.

KIKA: Say what?

MAGUE: Alicia, are you sure you're not on drugs?

KIKA: What's going on?

ALICIA: I'm...I'm...with Cathy.

KIKA: *Ay María purísima.*

(KIKA faints.)

ALICIA: Ama!

MAGUE: *Agua*; get her some water.

MARIA: You, *guera* get us some water.

ALICIA: Her name is Cathy.

CATHY: Not white girl.

ALICIA: She didn't mean it like that.

MARIA: Yes, I did.

ALICIA: No, you didn't.

MARIA: Just get us some water.

MAGUE: *Que* delicate.

ALICIA: *Ama*, wake up.

KIKA: *Dios mío.* I thought I heard you say you were with...

ALICIA: Cathy?

KIKA: Ay!

>   (SHE faints again.)

MARIA: Stop doing that.

ALICIA: Doing what?

MAGUE: *Muchacha malcriada.*

ALICIA: What did I do?

KIKA: OK, it's OK.

MARIA/ MAGUE: What!

KIKA: Maria, Maria, bring me an egg.

MARIA: *Si*, right away.

>   (SHE gets an egg from the fridge.)

Toma.

KIKA: Sit down.

ALICIA: That's not going to help...

MARIA/ MAGUE/KIKA: Sit down.

CATHY: What are they doing to you?

ALICIA: She's trying to cure me.

CATHY: From what?

ALICIA: *Ojo*?

KIKA: Someone must have put something on you. Have you been

feeling OK? Maybe that's why I've been feeling bad.

MARIA: Es brujería.

CATHY: What is that? I don't understand.

ALICIA: I'll explain later.

> (The doorbell rings.)

ALICIA: I'll get it.

> (SHE answers the door.)

It's the Jehovah's. They want to talk to you.

KIKA: That's not funny.

ALICIA: I'm not lying. Go see.

MARIA: It's a sign.

CATHY: Word travels fast.

KIKA: Tell them I'm not here.

ALICIA: But that would be a lie.

KIKA: Alicia! I don't have time for this.

ALICIA: OK.

> (KIKA rubs the egg all over ALICIA while all three
> women pray, preferably in Spanish.)

KIKA: Do you still have; are you still...

ALICIA: Yes.

KIKA: *Ay*, bring me a dozen eggs.

MAGUE: We don't have a dozen. Maria ate them all. You want me to go see if the chicken laid eggs today?

KIKA: Bring me the whole chicken...wait; bring me the candle of *la virgen* instead.

ALICIA: *Ama*, sit down. It isn't going to help. Nobody put anything on me.

KIKA: Let me try it again. Cathy, please, I'm sorry but I'm going to have to ask you to wait outside.

MAGUE: *Muchacha cochina...*

ALICIA: *Tía MAGUE*! Please stop. It isn't her fault. It's nobody's fault.

MARIA: It is your fault *hija*. God didn't intend for you to be like this.

CATHY: Science has proven...

MARIA: God said no!

CATHY: Will you say something?

ALICIA: Please be nice to her.

KIKA: I will take you to *Juana*; she will know how to cure you.

MARIA: Can we go eat first?

MAGUE: She retired member.

KIKA: We have to find someone.

MAGUE: What about *el señor López*! They say he has visions.

MARIA: Well of course he has visions, *si es un mariguano*!

MAGUE: Ah...no wonder he always looks so happy...*si, si muy alegre*.

KIKA: We'll have to get back to you but don't worry we will find someone.

ALICIA: *Ama...*

KIKA: Let's eat. I made enchiladas. Cathy, do you like en-chi-la-das?

CATHY: Yes.

MARIA: La vas a dejar que se quede aquí?

KIKA: Y que quieres que haga? Viajaron diez horas y apenas acaban de llegar.

MAGUE: No se tiene que ir Alicia. Solamente mandala a ella!

ALICIA: She understands some Spanish.

CATHY: I studied abroad.

MAGUE: *Pues, Válgame.*

CATHY: It's ok. I planned on staying in a hotel. It was nice to meet you.

ALICIA: I'll be back.

    (ALICIA and CATHY exit.)

MARIA: You need to do something right away. God doesn't accept these people into heaven. If you want to save her soul...

MAGUE: We get it.

MARIA: *Pues,* I was just saying.

MAGUE: Isn't God supposed to forgive people?

MARIA: If you confess your sins and promise not to do it again.

MAGUE: My God is about love.

MARIA: What God? You don't even go to church.

KIKA: Stop fighting; it doesn't do us any good.

MARIA: I saw this coming... we should have known cause...

KIKA: Don't say another word.

MARIA: I'm just saying.

KIKA: Well don't just say.

MARIA: Fine, I'm gonna go to the church and light some candles for her. You should do the same.

END OF SCENE

SCENE THREE

SETTING: A stage.

AT RISE: ZEREDA is on stage.

ZEREDA: And the three old ladies went on a search for a spiritual healer to cure the poor little lesbian of "the gay". They searched high and low, far and wide. They called all their friends; they called all their relatives. They looked in the mountains and they searched the river and all they found was some illegals building a wall. But give up they did not! Meanwhile trouble was brewing among the young lovebirds. Their love, they will soon find, will be tested to its borders.

   (CATHY and ALICIA enter.)

CATHY: I can't believe you let your family talk to me like that.

ALICIA: What was I supposed to do?

CATHY: My family doesn't treat you like that.

ALICIA: It's different.

CATHY: How?

ALICIA: They're white.

CATHY: Excuse me?

ALICIA: They're just more accepting. I mean, come on...you call your mom Tracy. My family just doesn't understand. I told you it was a bad idea.

CATHY: So, you wanted us to be a secret forever?

ALICIA: Not for forever.

CATHY: I'm proud to be with you.

ALICIA: I just need some time.

CATHY: I've given you a year.

ALICIA: Maybe I should take you back and come stay with them for a few days by myself.

CATHY: That's exactly what they want.

ALICIA: This is serious. They are looking for a healer to cure me.

CATHY: Please, don't tell me you believe in that stuff; that witchcraft.

ALICIA: It's not witchcraft.

CATHY: Those people are con-artists.

ALICIA: That's not true. I've seen it myself.

CATHY : You've seen what?

ALICIA: When I was little, we went to see this indigenous man somewhere deep in Mexico and he cured my dad's friend. My dad's friend could only walk with crutches and after he saw the guy he didn't need them anymore.

CATHY: He was probably part of the plan.

ALICIA: It's not fake...not all of it. I can't believe that. I mean, I spent my childhood in a car going to *curanderos* and visiting places where *la Virgen de Guadalupe* had appeared.

CATHY: It's just not logical.

ALICIA: Just drop it.

CATHY: Well, I don't want that stuff in our new apartment.

ALICIA: That stuff?

CATHY: I just don't get how you believe in that. I mean you're educated.

ALICIA: You're educated...you just overlook your mom's indiscretions.

CATHY: What indiscretions?

ALICIA: Drop it. I gotta call Zereda.

CATHY: For what?

ALICIA: She's been through this.

CATHY: You know how I feel about them.

ALICIA: Please go wait in the hotel. I'll be there soon.

CATHY: Don't be long. I love you.

ALICIA: I love you too.

ZEREDA: I've always wanted a nice young white boy....a Republican even. Someone from...let's see what do you have around here...Ft. Davis (Insert appropriate town or part of town). I can just picture me at dinner with his family...uh-huh yes, I agree with what President Bush said in his speech. Damn border jumpers...my family crossed the river on jet skis, uh-huh we're Spanish. (Jumping up) And then out of nowhere I'll strike with this speech...like our ancestors the Aztec warriors, we will rise to reclaim what is rightfully ours and we will call it Aztlan!...could you pass me the mashed potatoes, Tracy? Thanks hun. And by the way, Charles, Tracy's fucking Manuel...this is a fabulous meatloaf.

END OF SCENE

SCENE FOUR

SETTING: KIKA's kitchen.

AT RISE: MAGUE is waiting in the dark. ALICIA enters.

MAGUE: Alicia.

ALICIA: Hello?

MAGUE: Shh! Turn off the lights.

ALICIA: What's wrong? Is it *Ama*?

MAGUE: No, everything is OK. I just wanted to talk to you.

ALICIA: It's not a choice.

MAGUE: I know *mija*. I know. It's about your mother.

ALICIA: What about her?

MAGUE: Your mother had a...this friend that she was really close to; really close to. Ques que sleep overs...

ALICIA: Are you saying my mom was...

MAGUE: I'm not saying anything. You're grandpa hated her, the friend

ALICIA: Why?

MAGUE: Cause everybody knew that she was a...you know.

ALICIA: I don't understand.

MAGUE: I'm just saying that your grandma is really worried cause she doesn't want you to be like your mom. Your mom was living in a whole different world; a world that none of us understood.

ALICIA: How can I be like my mom? She was a drug addict.

MAGUE: Who told you that?

ALICIA: It's a small town.

MAGUE: I'm sorry *mija*. I know you're angry. You didn't deserve a mom like that.

ALICIA: Did my dad know?

MAGUE: I'm sure.

ALICIA: Is that why he left?

MAGUE: I don't know.

ALICIA: What was her name?

MAGUE: Who?

ALICIA: The girl; the friend; what was her name?

MAGUE: Alice.

(Cell phone is heard. THEY both check their phones.)

ALICIA: *Tía MAGUE* I didn't know you texted.

MAGUE: *Pues si.* What you think only you young ones can? Did you get that forward about the Mexican word of the day?

ALICIA: You sent that?

MAGUE: My favorite was the one about the wheelchair. *Mija*, we only have one burrito but it's OK cause we'll chair!

ALICIA: Gotta go back to the hotel.

MAGUE: Things will work out.

ALICIA: Do you think I'm bad?

MAGUE: It's not my life to judge.

ALICIA: Do you think it's a sin?

MAGUE: *No se.*

ALICIA: Do you think I can be cured?

MAGUE: Do you want to be cured?

ALICIA: I don't know.

MAGUE: It's all about faith.

(Phone is heard again. THEY both check.)

END OF SCENE

SCENE FIVE

SETTING: A stage.

AT RISE: STARKISHA, STARLINDA walk in to meet ZEREDA carrying a large amount of luggage.

STARKISHA: This is some Santeria ass shit.

STARLINDA: But it's true! My grandma told me...uh-huh she "seented" it.

STARKISHA: Well, we're here...lets clean up this hot mess.

STARLINDA: Girl, that is a pink ass shirt you're wearing.

STARKISHA: It's fuchsia.

STARLINDA: Its *chingame-la-vista* is what it is.

ZEREDA: Children...we have a job to do. Just when the little Mexican girl thought there was no way out, her drag mother came to her side. You see every little gay boy and girl has her very own drag mother.

STARKISHA: We're in training.

STARLINDA: We don't have our crowns.

ZEREDA: And let me tell you, we ain't no fairy godmothers...we get down. So, if you see us coming, give us a drink...

STARLINDA: Or a bump...

ZEREDA: And move outta the way biatch.

STARKISHA: I know that's right.

ZEREDA: Drag mothers endure years and years of training before we get our crowns.

STARLINDA: There should be another word for what we endure.

STARKISHA: I know that's right.

ZEREDA: But we don't give up.

STARLINDA: Nuh-uh, like that time that that stupid football player was making fun of me and pushing me until finally I beat the crap out of him. Sure did...with my little pony lunch box.

STARKISHA: Ooh girl, I can just see all your make-up flying all over the place.

STARLINDA: Speaking of make-up... what does a fashionable drag queen wear for such an occasion? It's my first time.

STARKISHA: Step one in our mission...watch The Dukes of Hazard.

ZEREDA: For what?

STARKISHA: Research. How else will we know what farmers wear?

ZEREDA: Were they farmers on that show?

STARLINDA: All I know is those two boys were hot!

ZEREDA: Hmmmm...still, that's the wrong look, and Alicia's family doesn't farm.

STARKISHA: But aren't they migrant workers or something?

STARLINDA: Oh hell no!

ZEREDA: Not every Mexican works in the fields.

STARLINDA: See, that's why we can't take you anywheres.

STARKISHA: Are they at least ranchers? I saw Bonanza. Ooh, ooh, I loved Urban Cowboy.

ZEREDA: No, no, and no.

STARKISHA: Then, how do we dress?

STARLINDA/ STARKISHA (Look at each other and have the same idea.): Sundresses!

ZEREDA (Checking a text.): Two hours later she texts me back.

STARKISHA: I hate that. If I text "hey" it's not ok to text "hey" back two hours later.

STARLINDA: I hate when people text me when they're in the restroom. *Cochinos, marranos, 'tascados!*

ZEREDA: OK girls, go put our stuff in the hotel. STARKISHA can you check the corn rows on my black wig? Thanks, hun.

STARKISHA: Why it gotta be me?

STARLINDA: Don't look at me?

STARKISHA: I just don't see why it's always gotta be me?

STARLINDA: I can make two braids like *La India Maria.*

STARKISHA: Fine, I'll do it.

(STARKISHA and STARLINDA exit.)

ZEREDA: Awww...I remember a time before I had my crown... when I was just a boy in heels with my mom's base and my sister's tank top. It was blue...with little rhinestones...she had bedazzled the shit out of it! Lets bring that back!

END OF SCENE

SCENE SIX

SETTING: KIKA's kitchen.

AT RISE: CATHY and ALICIA are arguing.

ALICIA: Yes, ok. I get it.

CATHY: No, you don't Alice. I don't want them here.

ALICIA: They're my friends. I said I would take your feelings into consideration...taken.

CATHY: Nothing good ever comes out of you hanging out with them. Why can't you just see that I only want the best for you?

ALICIA: I can't see something if it's shoved up in my face.

(There is a knock at the door.)

ALICIA: Can't just send them back now.

CATHY: They better not have brought anything with them.

(ZEREDA, STARLINDA, and STARKISHA enter.)

ZEREDA: We're here! We're queer! So are you!

STARKISHA: I know that's right.

STARLINDA: Uh-huh.

ZEREDA: Hi Cathy.

CATHY: Hi.

ZEREDA: Don't worry; we didn't bring our fairy dust.

CATHY: I wasn't worried.

ZEREDA: Uh-huh. How's your mom?

CATHY: She's good. Wait, you don't know my mom.

STARLINDA: Manuel does.

CATHY: Who's Manuel?

ZEREDA: Ignore her...she has jet lag.

CATHY: You drove...

ZEREDA: I simply asked about your mom to be polite. I took the liberty of assuming you have one.

CATHY: Oh.

ALICIA: OK. We don't have time for this; my grandma will be back soon. Help.

STARLINDA: What's going on *papis chulo*? Talk to us.

ALICIA: I came out to my grandma...

STARKISHA: Now why in the name of Jessie Jackson would you do that?

CATHY: She can't live her life in the closet.

ZEREDA: I don't know about you honey but the inside of my closet is fabulous.

STARKISHA: I know that's right.

STARLINDA: Is that all you ever say?

STARKISHA: What's wrong with it?

STARLINDA: You never add anything...you're not really saying anything.

STARKISHA: I'm just saying.

STARLINDA: No, you're not, that's the point.

STARKISHA: Rude.

CATHY: And this is who is going to solve everything for you?

STARLINDA: Excuse me!

ZEREDA: Bring it back to why we're here. What happened?

ALICIA: Well, I told her and my aunts...

STARLINDA: You told your whole family?

ALICIA: They were here.

STARKISHA: You could have waited.

ALICIA: You don't understand...they are never not here.

ZEREDA: What did they say?

ALICIA: My grandma passed out.

STARKISHA: Oh snap.

ZEREDA: So, she didn't take it well?

ALICIA: Not at all.

ZEREDA: And your aunts?

ALICIA: Well, my *tía María* is very, very religious.

STARKISHA: What did she say?

CATHY: God said no!

STARKISHA: Excuse me?

CATHY: That's what she said; God said no.

ALICIA: They want to take me to a *curandera*.

STARLINDA: Ay, no.

STARKISHA: Santeria ass shit!

CATHY: Please don't tell me you believe in that too?

STARLINDA: Uh, yes!

CATHY: You people are...

STARKISHA: You people? What do you mean you people? Don't include me. Its cause I'm Black isn't it?

CATHY: No! Of course not.

STARKISHA: What? I'm not Black enough, huh?

CATHY: No.

STARKISHA: No? Am I not ghetto enough?

CATHY: What? Stop twisting my words.

STARKISHA: I'll cut a bitch.

CATHY: Bitch?

STARKISHA: Bitch?

ALICIA: Please, stop. Ok? Please.

ZEREDA: It's ok *Papis*, we'll take care of it.

ALICIA: What are we gonna do?

ZEREDA (Pacing): Hmm...hmmm. We can...no, that won't work.

STARKSIHA: I don't know about this. I have a bad feeling in my stomach.

STARLINDA: Its the five tacos you ate.

STARKISHA: I feel it in my gut.

STARLINDA: The five tacos?

STARKISHA: Bitch.

STARLINDA: Bitch?

STARKISHA: Bitch.

ALICIA: Stop!

ZEREDA: Who has Joe's number?

STARLINDA: Don't go there!

ALICIA: What?

ZEREDA: We're going to set up our own shop.

STARKISHA: Our own shop? What do you mean our own shop? What kind of shop?

ZERENDA: A *curandera…curandero* shop!

STARKISHA: Cura what?

ZEREDA: When are they taking you?

STARKISHA: That's some voodoo ass shit!

ALICIA: I guess as soon as they find someone.

STARKISHA: Ain't nobody else scared?

ZEREDA: You mean as soon as they find us?

ALICIA: I'm scared.

ZEREDA: How many drag pageants have I put on?

STARLINDA: A lot.

ZEREDA: Yes indeed.

STARKISHA: This is not no pageant.

STARLINDA: Miss West Texas, Miss West Texas US of A, Miss West Texas at Large, Miss Cinco de Mayo, Miss Cinco de Mayo with Extra Tamales...

CATHY: I think we get it.

STARKISHA: Why doesn't anybody ever listen to the Black person in the room?

ZEREDA: Do you guys remember when I went to Houston to compete for the Miss Texas US of A?

ALICIA: Is that where you earned your crown?

ZEREDA: No, I didn't win.

STARLINDA: She didn't come back empty handed though.

STARKISHA: Nuh-huh...girl, brought herself back a case of the herpes.

STARLINDA: I think it was more like gonoherpasyphilitys.

STARKISHA: Girl had herself a good time.

STARLINDA: *Perra*!

ZEREDA: Enough! Starlinda and Starkisha will find us a place. I'll call Joe and tell him to get here ASAP.

ALICIA: What do I do?

CATHY: You don't actually think this is going to work, do you?

ALICIA: We don't have a choice.

CATHY: Yes, we do. This is crazy.

ZEREDA: *Mija*, if you are going to be with a Chicana you are going to need to understand that sometimes we do a whole lot of crazy ass shit that we don't understand or maybe believe, but we do it anyways because our *abuela* said so ok? Ok?

STARLINDA: Ok?

CATHY: Well that's not how we do things.

STARLINDA: Esta cabrona.

ZEREDA: Well you better start getting used to it honey because soon there will be more of us than more of you. We're making more babies and climbing more walls than you can imagine. Start eating tamales and getting tattoos of Selena because here we come. Ok? Ok.

ALICIA: So, what is it that you want me to do?

ZEREDA: Buy us some time.

ALICIA: How much time? What if they find someone else?

ZEREDA: You can tell them you found someone as soon as I get a hold of Joe.

CATHY: That is the most ridiculous idea ever.

STARLINDA: No hunny, thinking that those shoes go with that outfit is the most ridiculous idea.

CATHY: Ugh!

STARLINDA: You ugh.

CATHY: Can you please grow up?

STARLINDA: Can you not be a pretentious ass bi...

ALICIA: Hey, hey...

CATHY: Oh my, that's a big word for you.

ZEREDA: That's enough out of both of you.

STARLINDA: She started it. *Ay Alicia, no se que miras en esta gringa chingada.*

CATHY: English. This is the US.

STARLINDA: And before that it was Mexico and before that it was *Aztlán* and one day it will return to *Aztlán!* You just wait and see. We rising up.

STARKISHA: You get it girl! Back to our roots...but I ain't going back to no Africa...its too damn hot.

STARLINDA: Girl, it be hot everywhere. This global warming...

CATHY: Leave then. Go find your *Aztlán.*

STARLINDA: *Babosa,* I am in *Aztlán.*

CATHY: You are in the United States.

STARLINDA: My grandma always said I shouldn't stoop down to anyone's level and talk bad about them...in English...*pinche puta jodida hija de tu chingada madre!*

STARKISHA: Bless you.

    (EVERYONE looks at Starkisha)

STARKISHA: What? I don't know what she's saying.

ZEREDA: As entertaining as this all is, we have work to do if we're going to pull this off. You two kiss and make up and we'll go find a place to open up shop.

    (THEY exit.)

ALICIA: I'm so sorry.

CATHY: It's not your fault your friends are ghetto.

ALICIA: They're not ghetto.

CATHY: Yes, they are. When are you going to leave all this behind?

ALICIA: I can't just forget where I came from.

CATHY: Well, you better pay attention to where you're going.

END OF SCENE

SCENE SEVEN

SETTING: KIKA's kitchen.

AT RISE: ZEREDA is on stage.

ZEREDA: Doesn't she have a fabulous tan? You know, I don't understand why white people oppress us and then tan so they can look like us!

> (KIKA, MAGUE, and MARIA are sitting at the kitchen table drinking coffee and going through phone books, a Rolodex, and box full of little pieces of paper.)

MAGUE: *Mira, aqui encontre una señora que cura. Se llama* sister Sofia. *Le llamamos?*

MARIA: *Sofia?* Hmm…*Sofia*…no, doesn't sound like a *curandera's* name.

KIKA: Nope.

MAGUE: And what does a *curandera's* name sound like?

MARIA: Not like *Sofia*.

KIKA: Nope.

MAGUE: Fine. Who did you find?

KIKA: Nobody. I've called everyone.

MARIA: What about that lady in…

KIKA: Nope.

MARIA: You don't even know what I was going to say.

KIKA: Yes, I do.

MARIA: No.

KIKA: *Carmen.*

MARIA: How did you know?

KIKA: I just did.

MAGUE: Maybe you're a *curandera*?

KIKA: *No seas payasa.* I already told you no; she's not from a good family.

MARIA: *Pero* these are desperate times. *Alicia's* a...

KIKA: She's not. She's just confused.

MAGUE: What do you mean by she's not from a good family?

KIKA: Her family and our family are both from *El Guante.* When they moved there it was only 3 women. *Se nos hizo raro que* they were alone. We had heard *que* they had been kicked out of their last village.

MAGUE: Por que?

KIKA: *Eran brujas.*

MAGUE: *Brujas?*

KIKA: *Yo tampoco lo creia...de primero.* But one of our brothers *se enamoro de una de las hijas.*

MAGUE: His wife was one of those *brujas?*

KIKA: *No, la dejo cuando se enamoro de su primera esposa, Rosa.*

MAGUE: *Oh.*

KIKA: Esta tan enojada. Y le dijo que se iba a arrepentir y que no le iba a durar el amor.

MAGUE: Que no se murió la primera esposa?

KIKA: *Si.* When she was giving birth she was yelling that she couldn't breath and she couldn't breath and she didn't make it.

MARIA: And standing at the door was the mother.

MAGUE: Of the *brujas?*

KIKA: Yes! And *Rosa's* neck was red.

MARIA: You could see the handprints.

MAGUE: Que feo.

KIKA: Do you still want me to ask her?

MARIA: No.

MAGUE: How is she related to them?

KIKA: *Es prima.*

MAGUE: Why couldn't *Alicia* at least find a nice Mexican girl?

MARIA: She shouldn't even be with a girl.

MAGUE: *Pues no* but, at least she could have found a *Mexicana...a Latina...*Puerto Rican, *Colombiana...*

KIKA: No, they sell drugs.

MAGUE: No *todas.* A *Cubana...*

MARIA: We get it...a Latina.

MAGUE: *Pues*, I'm just saying.

    (ALICIA enters.)

ALICIA: Saying what?

KIKA: Nothing *mija*.

MAGUE: Why you couldn't be with a nice Mexican?

MARIA: Boy.

MAGUE: Most importantly Mexican...

MARIA/KIKA: Boy.

MARIA: Tiene dinero?

ALICIA: Tía.

MARIA: Does she?

    (ALICIA receives a text.)

ALICIA: Not really.

MARIA: What does not really mean?

ALICIA: Her parents have money.

MARIA: Well, at least there's that.

ALICIA: I said her parents have money; not her.

MARIA: When they die she gets it.

ALICIA: Tía!

MAGUE: What do her parents do?

KIKA: Que importa?

MAGUE: We need to know what kind of family she comes from?

KIKA: A white family.

ALICIA: *Ama,* what does it matter that they are white?

KIKA: They don't think the same as us...they're not the same. It might be ok for their daughter to be gay but it's not ok for us.

MAGUE: They are different.

MARIA: Uh-huh.

MAGUE: They fart in public.

MARIA: Uh-huh.

MAGUE: *Como si nada*...they just say excuse me...*descarados...no tienen vergüenza.*

ALICIA: Well, what are you suppose to say?

KIKA: This is what I was afraid of; you're turning into one of them. That's why I didn't want you to go off to that college.

MAGUE: You could have stayed here.

ALICIA: They don't have what I want to study.

KIKA: *Que quieres* study?

ALICIA: Fashion merchandising.

MAGUE: *Pero,* you don't have fashion.

ALICIA: Just cause you don't like it doesn't mean it's not fashionable. This is fashionable to us.

MAGUE: What's the point of paying good money for torn pants? When we were little they made fun of us for wearing torn pants.

ALICIA: It's just not like that anymore.

KIKA: I knew I shouldn't have let you go. You are coming back.

ALICIA: I can't just quit in the middle of the semester.

KIKA: Then you'll come back as soon as it's over.

ALICIA: I'm not coming back.

KIKA: Yes, you are!

ALICIA: It's not fair! I'm doing good.

MARIA: You call this good?

ALICIA: I'm sorry *tía* but this really is none of your business.

KIKA: Alicia!

ALICIA: Well its not.

KIKA: You have to choose. Us or them.

ALICIA: I can't believe you're doing this.

KIKA: You did this. *No lo puedo creer.*

ALICIA: What if I change?

KIKA: Change how?

MARIA: Leave her.

ALICIA: If I'm not with her can I stay?

KIKA: I'll think about it.

MARIA: Are you still going to church?

ALICIA: Yes.

MARIA: Then just pray to God *mija*...he will help you.

KIKA: Enough. We need to find you some help.

ALICIA: I found someone.

MAGUE: Who?

ALICIA: His name is Jose. He's new.

MAGUE: Where's he from?

ALICIA: I don't know. I think somewhere in Mexico.

KIKA: Where is he?

ALICIA: Here in town.

KIKA: Here in town where?

ALICIA: Over in that new neighborhood. He lives with his son.

KIKA: Donde cura?

ALICIA: Allí en su casa, en un cuartito atrás.

KIKA: Let's take you then.

ALICIA: Right now?

KIKA: Yes, right now.

ALICIA: We can't.

KIKA: Why?

MAGUE: We probably need to call first.

ALICIA: Yes, we do. We need to call first.

KIKA: Then call.

ALICIA: Right now?

KIKA: Yes, right now!

ALICIA: Ok, don't get mad.

KIKA: Pues, me desesperas!

ALICIA: Ok, I'll call.

KIKA: Where are you going?

ALICIA: Outside to call.

KIKA: Why can't you call here in front of us?

MAGUE: Ya, déjala.

ALICIA: No, that's fine tía. What do I say?

KIKA: Pregúntale que si te pude dar una limpia.

(SHE calls.)

ALICIA: Bueno. Esta el señor José? Gracias. Bueno...quería saber si podía venir a verlo para que me de una limpia. A bueno si...no, lo entiendo?

KIKA: Que dijo?

ALICIA: *Que viniera mañana en la tarde.*

KIKA: *A que horas?*

ALICIA: Después de las cinco.

KIKA: *Bueno.*

ALICIA: I'll be back tomorrow?

KIKA: Where are you going?

ALICIA: To the hotel.

KIKA: I think you should stay here. I don't want you to see that girl anymore.

ALICIA: You're gonna get what you want soon so just leave me alone for now.

KIKA: What has happened to you? What world are you living in? I didn't raise you like this!

ALICIA: I'll see you tomorrow.

(SHE exits.)

MARIA: Válgame! Esa muchacha...

KIKA: Es porque anda allá con todos esos gringos.

MAGUE: Don't be like that...it's not the white's people fault that she's...you know...

KIKA: *Pero* they're just out in the open?

MAGUE: Maybe they're not...maybe we're not so different?

KIKA: Did you think that when we were working every summer and they were in their trucks?

MAGUE: No.

KIKA: Ok, then.

MAGUE: But that girl wasn't the one who treated us bad. Her parents didn't do anything to us. Lots of things have changed.

KIKA: Todos son iguales! Todavía tienen el poder. No es verdad que nos miran como iguales.

MAGUE: I never knew you thought like this.

KIKA: Now you do.

MAGUE: What if you push Alicia too far? What if we loose her?

KIKA: So I should let her ruin her life just like *Lidia*?

MAGUE: You need to let that go. Sheltering Alicia won't bring her back.

MARIA: Maybe we should go to church to light candles?

END OF ACT

ACT TWO

SCENE ONE

SETTING: A small, plain room. With a few seats and a table.

AT RISE: ZEREDA is on stage as the appropriate scene change takes place.

ZEREDA: Everyone still with me? Good. Let's move this story right along...we know you can only take so much cultural enrichment for one day. Just like church...get to the point; tell me what Jesus said. That's what I like about the Catholic church...you get a good priest and you're in and out in forty-five minutes and they wine and dine you. Stand, sit, kneel,
"Jesus said no"...thanks for the wine and guilt...see you in a week!

> (CATHY and JOE enter and begin placing candles all over
> the room and preparing an altar.)

CATHY: I don't understand how this is going to work.

JOE: Trust me. I've been to lots of these *curanderos.* And I'm a theatre major.

CATHY: This isn't a play.

JOE: Sure it is. I like to think that the set represents...

CATHY: You can tell me later. We don't have very long to get ready. This really is ridiculous.

JOE: I did the best I could.

CATHY: How did you get this place?

JOE: I know this guy who has a crazy uncle who served in Vietnam with limping Arturo, who has a daughter that dated my cousin Junior who gave her one of my dog's puppies, who owes me a favor.

CATHY: So, it's her house?

JOE: No, she has an aunt who has a daughter *que salio mal* because she went to the lake...Wait, do you hear that?

CATHY: No, what?

JOE: What?

CATHY: What? What?

JOE: I guess it was nothing. Oh, it belongs to her baby's daddy's uncle.

CATHY: This must be a Mexican thing.

JOE: What's a Mexican thing?

CATHY: I know this guy, Adam who knows everybody! Anything you need...he knows someone who knows someone who can get it.

JOE: Adam! He wears that one cap all the time and has a goatee and hangs out with Juan who carries a cell phone that always disconnected?

CATHY: I don't know.

JOE: Yeah, I bet it's him. No, it's not a Mexican thing. That's how it works in Washington too. Some idiot knows another idiot whose dad owns a whole bunch of oil companies who owes this other guy a favor cause he got his son into Yale.

CATHY: Ok, well let's just keep moving along shall we?

JOE: Yes, cause I'll need time to get into costume.

CATHY: Where did you get all this stuff?

JOE: My grandma's house.

CATHY: Isn't she gonna notice it's gone?

JOE: She has more.

CATHY: More?

JOE: Lots more.

CATHY: I'm kinda scared.

JOE: Of all the stuff?

CATHY: No! This is all just weird.

JOE: I guess I can see how it would be weird to you.

CATHY: Do you believe in it?

JOE: Yeah.

CATHY: I'm just going along with all this cause I know how hard this has been for Alice.

JOE: I didn't even know she was planning on telling her grandma.

CATHY: We've been talking about it for a while.

JOE: I see.

CATHY: What?

JOE: What, what?

CATHY: Why do you say it like that? All, "I see?"

JOE: I just never thought that Alicia was ever going to tell her.

CATHY: Why wouldn't she?

JOE: Her grandma's all she has. Are you out to your family?

CATHY: They've known since I was in the seventh grade.

JOE: *Perdón!* Get it girl!

CATHY: What if something goes wrong?

JOE: What can possibly go wrong?

CATHY: What if you accidentally cure her?

JOE: Girl please! It would take Jesus Christ himself to come down and cure that lesbian.

CATHY: What if they figure out you're fake?

JOE: They won't.

CATHY: I can't believe she's going through with this.

JOE: Remind me how you guys met again?

CATHY: I was taking a multi cultural class...

JOE: And she was your research project?

CATHY: Yeah. I mean no. What?

JOE: Ummhmm...I bet what.

CATHY: Regardless of how we met...I fell in love with her.

JOE: What do you love about her?

CATHY: Everything. Her eyes, her body, her hair, her skin tone... everything.

JOE: Yeah, that sounds like everything.

(Voices are heard off stage.)

CATHY: What's that?

JOE: What?

CATHY: That.

JOE: I got my friends to come in.

CATHY: For what?

JOE: Extras.

CATHY: We don't need extras!

JOE: It needs to look legitimate.

CATHY: All your friends are either flaming or drag queens.

JOE: Your point is?

CATHY: You barely even look straight.

JOE: Your point is?

CATHY: We won't be able to fool anybody.

JOE: Walter Mercado was loved by millions of Latinos hunny and he was the biggest queen of all of them?

CATHY: Who?

JOE: Really? You have no culture. We need to get ready.

CATHY: No! Tell them to leave.

JOE: All of them?

CATHY: Yes.

JOE: Even the pretty ones?

>   (SHE nods her head yes.)
Fine.

>   (HE walks out and is heard off stage.)

JOE: OK people. We don't need you after all. Don't forget auditions on Tuesday.

(The crowd is heard leaving. As the noise of the crowd is diminishing we hear ZEREDA.)

ZEREDA: Hey…Alizé, how you been girl? You looking good…love the new nose. Hey, Ecstasy…you doing Miss West Texas US of A… at Large?

(ZEREDA, STARKISHA, and STARLINDA enter.)

STARKISHA: Ecstasy? Shit, she ain't even Tylenol!

ZEREDA: (To Cathy) Excuse me sir….sir, sir, sir…

CATHY: What!

ZEREDA: Can you tell us where the dressing rooms are?

CATHY: This is not a show!

STARKISHA: Girl, you need to calm down.

STARLINDA: Umm hmm, that ponytail must be a little too tight.

STARKISHA: OK, sweetie let's start all over again…like new. I'm Starkisha Neveah Raven.

STARLINDA: And, I'm Starlinda Neveah Raven.

ZEREDA: And I'm…

CATHY: Star Jones!

ZEREDA: Oh no she didn't! Damn lesbian thinks she has jokes.

STARLINDA: They all do. It's the whole Ellen craze.

STARKISHA: Girl be getting it with that hot ass wife of hers though.

47

ZEREDA: Like I was saying...I'm Zereda, their drag mother.

STARLINDA: We don't have our crowns yet.

JOE: *Perras*! It's nice to see you girls.

STARLINDA: What can we help with *Papis*?

JOE: We still have a lot to do...can you help me get the big picture of *La Virgen* from the back?

STARLINDA: As long as it's big and from the back...

      (JOE, ZEREDA and STARLINDA exit.)

CATHY: I don't understand the whole drag queen thing.

STARKISHA: I'm not a sideshow honey.

CATHY: Do you really like to dress like that?

STARKISHA: Do you really like being a truck driver?

CATHY: Are all drag queens this rude?

STARKISHA: Are all lesbians this plain?

CATHY: You have really big feet.

STARKISHA: You know what they say about queens with big feet?

CATHY: What?

STARKISHA: We go through a lot of tape.

CATHY: What is it with the tape? I don't get it.

STARKISHA: You wouldn't.

CATHY: We have a job to do.

STARKISHA: Baby I don't mean to be rude but...what you doing up in Alicia's world?

CATHY: What do you mean?

STARKISHA: Baby I know your type...liberal acting, granola loving, gluten hating, mountain hiking, Europe back-packing, I wanna save you from your oppression.

CATHY: I think that Alice has a lot of potential and she deserves better.

STARKISHA: Deserves better than what? This neighborhood? Her family? Her education?

CATHY: What would you know about education?

STARKISHA: I know how to cut you, dump you in the desert, and make it look like you were an innocent victim of this damn drug problem we are having.

CATHY: Is that a threat?

STARKISHA: Baby queens make promises.

CATHY: I'm not even going to be bothered by you. Alice knows what's important to her. She knows where she is headed in life. I don't have to justify my relationship to you.

STARKISHA: No, you don't. I just see you struggling. You shouldn't have to work so hard if its true love baby.

CATHY: How long have you been married? That's what I thought.

STARKISHA: I'm just saying that there needs to be more than that sexual attraction thang you got going. I guess I might just be being a little unfair....still feeling a little sensitive about all these years of white oppression.

CATHY: Oppression? You have a black president for God's sake.

SATRKISHA: Baby he is half white, you better claim your half.

(They continue to get things ready)

I like that little number you have on.

CATHY: Thanks. I like your dress too.

STARKISHA: Well thank you. It doesn't make me look fat does it?

CATHY: Not at all.

STARKISHA: Maybe you are good for Alicia after all.

CATHY: Where do you buy your dresses?

STARKISHA: Online.

CATHY: Oooh on what site?

STARKSIHA: Oh no honey, a queen will never reveal her sources.

CATHY: Hmm. What size are you?

STARKISHA: I'm a size...well...I'm... I'm in the process of losing weight OK. I'm really trying...its hard to workout in heels!

(STARLINDA, ZEREDA and JOE enter.)

STARLINDA: (Consoling her.) What happened?

STARKISHA: She asked me what size dress I wore.

STARLINDA: It's OK baby girl. (To Cathy) What is your problem?

CATHY: What?

STARLINDA: You don't ask a queen that.

CATHY: Sorry.

STARLINDA: Girl, you look good. Don't listen to her.

STARKISHA: Really?

STARLINDA: Yes, you're beautiful.

>   (ALICIA rushes in.)

ALICIA: They're on their way. Hurry! Are you done?

CATHY: Are they outside?

ALICIA: Not yet, they were arguing with my *tía Maria* because she wanted to go eat first.

>   (THEY all run around for a few moments putting the
>
>   finishing touches on the room.)

I'm scared! What if something goes wrong?

ZEREDA: Everything will be ok.

ALICIA: Maybe we should pray.

STARLINDA: Good idea.

>   (THEY all get on their knees and do the sign of the cross.)

STARLINDA/STARKISHA/ZEREDA: Dear Selena.

CATHY: Oh, my, God. Seriously?

STARLINDA: She's our patron saint! She's done miracles and shit.

CATHY: Ok.

STARLINDA: Dear Selena please be with us and help us be *perras y trucha* in all we do.

STARKISHA: And give us good hair and highlights without roots.

STARLINDA/STARKISHA/ZEREDA: Amen.

(ALICIA exits.)

ZEREDA: Ok. Everyone go get in costume and places.

STARKISHA: Good thing I brought hair options.

STARLINDA: What's happening? What's going on? Why are you not getting ready?

ZEREDA: Baby a real queen is always ready. Write that down.

END OF SCENE

SCENE TWO

SETTING: A small waiting room with lots of religious candles and ornaments.

AT RISE: ZEREDA on stage. MARIA, KIKA, ALICIA, and MAGUE are heard outside.

ZEREDA: They're coming! What do you want me to do Joe?

> (CATHY runs off.)

JOE: Sit down and don't talk to them. Places!

ZEREDA: Why not?

JOE: Just. This is my show now.

ZEREDA: That's so butch.

> (ALICIA, KIKA, MARIA, and MAGUE enter ad-libbing.)

ALICIA: I think we should forget about this whole thing.

KIKA: Sit down.

ALICIA: I'm a little hungry. Let's go get something to eat.

MARIA: I have a *burrito* in my purse.

> (SHE pulls out and extremely large burrito and hands it
> to ALICIA.)

ALICIA: Thanks but I need some *chile*. We should go get some.

MARIA: I got some.

(SHE pulls a little jar of *chile* out of her purse.)

ALICIA: Thanks. I...

MARIA: I've got a spoon too if you need it.

(SHE pulls out a spoon.)

ALICIA: Thank you.

MAGUE: What else do you have in that purse?

MARIA: A *soda*, a candy, a *taco*, holy water and a *quequito*.

(SHE pulls out each item as she lists it.)

MAGUE: Can I have the *soda*?

MARIA: No.

MAGUE: The *quequito*?

MARIA: No.

MAGUE: How comes?

MARIA: It's mine.

MAGUE: Doesn't God say to share?

MARIA: God said no!

KIKA: Will you two please stop that? *Maria*, put your cafeteria away.

MARIA: *Ay*, how delicate.

KIKA: (Whispering to MAGUE and pointing at Zereda.) This girl is a little bit ugly, no?

MAGUE: She looks like this boy who used to live next door to me.

(JOE is heard from the other room.)

JOE: Next!

(*ZEREDA* gets up and walks into the other room.)

KIKA: There was something really weird about that lady.

MAGUE: *Si.*

MARIA: She's really tall?

MAGUE: And she has a lot of muscles.

ALICIA: She works out a lot.

MARIA: How do you know?

ALICIA: Cause. You can tell. I just know. Leave me alone.

MAGUE: How delicate.

KIKA: I hope they make her prettier.

ALICIA: *Ama!*

KIKA: Her make-up is horrible.

MAGUE: How comes you don't wear make-up?

MARIA: *Por que* she's gay!

MAGUE: Oh.

ALICIA: That's not why.

MARIA: Then why?

ALICIA: Because, I don't want to be objectified.

MARIA: *Que es eso?*

MAGUE: *No se.* You could use a little bit.

ALICIA: I wear make-up sometimes.

MAGUE: I mean you're pretty it's just...

ALICIA: I would look better.

MARIA: She's just saying.

MAGUE: (Pulling out a huge book.) I've been doing some research...are you butch or a...*como se dice*...chap stick, no, lipstick lesbian?

ALICIA: Tía!

KIKA: Que es eso?

ALICIA: Oh my God.

MAGUE: *Mira,* I found a guide; how to understand your gay, lesbian, bisexual, or transgender daughter.

KIKA: *Que es* transgender?

MAGUE: Here are some pictures. Which one are you?

ALICIA: Oh, God.

MARIA: At least she still believes in God.

KIKA: *Que es* transgender!

MAGUE: *Pues* according to this picture it looks like a girl that looks like a boy.

MARIA: Que dice ahí?

MAGUE: It says you can have an operation. There's another picture.

(The LADIES examine the picture. THEY turn the picture upside down as they slowly tilt their heads to the side.)

KIKA: *Dios mío!*

(SHE faints.)

ALICIA: Ama!

KIKA: What happened?

MARIA: You saw transgender.

(MAGUE shows her the picture again.)

MAGUE: Mira!

KIKA: Ay no!

(SHE faints again.)

ALICIA: Put the damn pictures away!

(*ZEREDA* walks out of the other room.)

ZEREDA: Excuse me. Let me see. Give me room. You have to give her air.

(SHE rests KIKA's head on her lap.)

ALICIA: I told you it was a bad idea.

JOE: Next!

ZEREDA: KIKA. KIKA. Wake up, honey. It's ok.

KIKA: What happened? Un ángel.

ZEREDA: No honey, I'm not an angel I'm…

ALICIA: Leaving! We're leaving.

JOE: Next!

KIKA: No, we're here to get you help. Let's go.

(All four LADIES get up.)

ALICIA: We can't all go in there.

KIKA: Why not?

ALICIA: Cause it will be too crowded.

KIKA: Then he can come out here.

ALICIA: I'll just go in by myself.

KIKA: No, we have to be there.

(JOE walks out.)

JOE: What's the problem out here?

MARIA: Can we all go in there?

JOE: No, it will be too crowded.

KIKA: Then you can do it out here.

ALICIA: I don't think he can.

JOE: I think I can.

ALICIA: No, you can't.

JOE: Yes, I can. What do you need help with?

ZEREDA: Tolerance.

(SHE exits.)

MAGUE: *Que es eso?*

MARIA: I think maybe it's a fungus.

KIKA: *Quien sabe.*

MAGUE: She's gay.

JOE: But what's the problem? Uh, I mean, how long have you felt this way?

ALICIA: As long as I can remember.

JOE: Have you tried dating men?

ALICIA: Yes.

JOE: And what happened?

ALICIA: Nothing.

JOE: Did you know about this?

KIKA: No!

MAGUE: I kind of thought so.

KIKA: What?

MARIA: She was a bit of a tomboy.

MAGUE: Yes.

MARIA: And she doesn't wear make-up.

ALICIA: That's enough.

JOE: I'm getting a strong vibe from the older ladies.

KIKA: What do you mean?

JOE: Are any of you gay?

MARIA/ MAGUE/ KIKA: No!

JOE: Hmm...let me go get my candle. Wait here just a minute.

(JOE exits. The women ad-lib. JOE walks back in with a candle.)

JOE: Does anyone have a lighter?

ALICIA: I think I might.

MAGUE: Do you smoke?

MARIA: Smoke!

KIKA: Who smokes?

ALICIA: No! I don't smoke. I don't have one.

MARIA: I think I might have one. Let me look.

(MARIA looks in her purse.)

Here's one. No wait. It's a hot pickle.

JOE: Ooh, what's a hot pickle?

MARIA: It's a pickle with *chile*.

KIKA: Put the cafeteria away!

JOE: I can feel it without lighting the candle. Let me just harness my chi.

MARIA: Pee! You're going to harness your pee?

JOE: No. Let's see...yes, I see now.

KIKA: What is it?

JOE: It is a gay spirit.

MAGUE: A what?

JOE: A gay spirit has entered your family. It was meant for one of you.

KIKA: It was those *brujas*! I know it. Was it?

JOE: Yes, yes it was.

MAGUE: Can we get rid of it?

JOE: It will be hard...be right back!

> (JOE exits. The women ad-lib. JOE walks back
> in with a bowl, a bottle of liquor, a bottle of holy water
> and matches.)

JOE: Ladies, please come stand over here. Not you Alicia.

KIKA: But she's the one that is...you know.

JOE: It's you they want.

> (JOE does a ridiculous ritual and prays.)

Padre nuestro que estas en el suelo. Santificado sea tu nombre. San, san, colita de rana. Ayuda a Alicia que no sea lesbiana.

KIKA: Did it work?

JOE: I'm afraid not.

KIKA: Then we'll take her somewhere else.

MAGUE: But then, what about us?

JOE: One of you is gay too!

KIKA: What are you saying?

ALICIA: You made me gay.

KIKA: *Ay Dios mio*!

(SHE faints.)

ALICIA: *Ama*!

(MARIA and MAGUE try to wake her up.)

KIKA: Is there anything we can do?

JOE: I'm afraid it's her destiny.

MARIA: It can't be.

JOE: It is her cross to bear.

MARIA: Oh.

KIKA: *Aye Dios*!

(SHE faints again.)

MAGUE: Again?

(The WOMEN try to wake her up with no success.)

ALICIA: Let's carry her out.

MARIA: *Ay no*, she's too heavy.

ALICIA: Maria!

MARIA: I guess we can try.

(The WOMEN gather their purses and begin to carry KIKA out.)

KIKA: Don't forget my purse.

MAGUE: I thought she was passed out.

ALICIA: *Ama*? Can you hear me? Hurry, let's just get her out of here.

(The WOMEN exit ad-libbing the entire time. JOE relaxes and begins to get out of costume. CATHY comes out from the back room. MAGUE rushes back in. CATHY quickly runs back.)

MAGUE: Do you have anything for weight loss? You know...I think I got the fat spirit.

JOE: Yes, take these herbal pills.

MAGUE: What is it?

JOE: You have to have faith.

ALICIA: (From off stage) Tia!

MAGUE: Thank you. Bye!

(SHE steals a candle on the way out. CATHY, ZEREDA, STARKISHA, and STARLINDA come out.)

CATHY: Whew, that was close.

STARLINDA: What did you give her?

JOE: Hydroxycut.

STARKISHA: That's gonna be one excited old lady.

CATHY: Is that even safe at her age?

JOE: I don't know...I was in the moment.

ALICIA: (Rushing in.) That was crazy.

CATHY: How's your grandma?

ALICIA: She'll be ok. They're gonna take her home to rest.

JOE: I'm surprised they let you out of their sight.

ALICIA: I told them I was going to the hotel to break up with you.

CATHY: What?

ALICIA: Not really. I just said that so they would let me go.

CATHY: But they are going to think that you broke up with me.

ALICIA: Yeah? But I'm not.

CATHY: You don't get it do you?

ALICIA: No?

CATHY: I've put up with enough crazy shit. I'm leaving…hope you find a ride back.

ZEREDA: Its ok baby, we're here for you.

STARKISHA: That sucks.

ALICIA: I love her guys! I know you don't understand…

ZEREDA: We do understand. She was your first.

ALICIA: Yes.

ZEREDA: And you think you'll never find anyone else who will ever love you.

ALICIA: Yes.

ZEREDA: And right now you're feeling insecure, and your chest feels tight, and you feel like you can't breath.

ALICIA: Yes.

STARKISHA: Baby, you're young. You can find someone else. How old are you?

ALICIA: Twenty.

STARKISHA: In lesbian years that's like thirty…see you're still young.

STARLINDA: My grandma always said, "When life gives you lemons pick'em up and hit the shit out of someone...*quien quiere* lemonade *a la chingada!*"

ALICIA: Maybe you're right; maybe I can find another girl.

ZEREDA: That's the spirit!

ALICIA: I can't!

STARLINDA: I know what you need. Music please and bring some beers.

> (A sad Norteño song such as *Tragos de Amargo Licor*
>   begins to play and JOE bring out beers. They all cry in
>   unison, drink, cry, drink...)

ALICIA: Por que? Por que?

STARLINDA: It's ok *Papis*. Just let it out.

ALICIA: Pinche puta jodida.

STARKISHA: This is just too sad...why? Why?

STARLINDA: Are you ok? This song gets you doesn't it?

STARKISHA: Yes...I don't really know what he's saying but I'm sure it's sad.

> (Voices are heard off stage.)

JOE: Do you hear that?

ALICIA: That's my grandma's voice.

JOE: Shit! Do they want another *limpia*?

ALICIA: You were supposed to return to Mexico.

> (THEY all scramble for a place to hide. KIKA,

MARIA, and MAGUE enter before they can hide. JOE screams as they get caught. The ladies are dressed really butch.)

MAGUE: Isn't that the *curandero*?

MARIA: Are you?

JOE: Hi...

KIKA: What's going on here, Alicia?

MAGUE: (To Zereda) I know where I remember you from...*ya se!*

MARIA: That's the ugly girl.

ZEREDA: E-cu-me!

MAGUE: That's *Chilo's* son!

(SHE takes off his wig.)

KIKA: Aye, Maria Purisima!

(*The three old LADIES do the sign of the cross.*)

KIKA: I thought you died?

ZEREDA: That's what my father told everybody.

MAGUE: Why?

ZEREDA: Cause I'm gay.

KIKA: You poor boy...girl...boy.

ZEREDA: Girl.

KIKA: Alicia, what is going on?

ALICIA: I asked Joe to pretend to be a *curandero*.

KIKA: Why?

ALICIA: Cause.

MARIA: You lied to us?

ALICIA: I had to. I didn't think you would love me anymore.

KIKA: You thought we didn't love you?

ALICIA: No.

KIKA: Look at us?

ALICIA: Yeah, why are you dressed like that?

KIKA: We thought if we accepted our fate it would save you.

JOE: I made that up.

KIKA: No, I really am gay.

ALICIA: No you're not!

KIKA: Yes, I am!

ALICIA: You can't be.

    (SHE faints.)

 KIKA: Alicia, mija!

JOE: *No mames,* you too!

ALICIA: But you were married and ...

KIKA: How do you like our joke?

ALICIA: What! What kind of a sick joke was that?

MAGUE: How does your own medicine taste?

KIKA: We're old but not stupid. How dare you think you could get away with a fake *curandero*?

MAGUE: That means something to us!

ALICIA: I'm sorry.
MARIA: I don't want anything to do with this world you have chosen. I shouldn't have even come back here.

KIKA: I hope you decide to come home.

    (MAGUE and KIKA exit.)

STARLINDA: My grandma always said that God doesn't ever give you more than you can handle. What? What did you think she said?

    (ALICIA exits.)

ZEREDA: In the end there isn't always a happily ever after.

STARLINDA: Did you know that 75% of gay people don't stay with their first?

STARKSIHA: Really?

STARLINDA: Well, I made up the 75% but I'm sure it's a lot. A lot!

STARKISHA: I know of one.

STARLINDA: Love one, heartbreak five billion.

STARKISHA: As long as there's one there's still hope.

ZEREDA: Hope is overrated honey. Reality is all that matters.

STARKSIHA: Is hope against the rules?

ZEREDA: No.

STARKSIHA: Then I'll keep hoping thank you very much.

ZEREDA: I like that about you. And you know love doesn't just hide from the gays. These poor straight people struggle too.

STARLINDA: Really?

ZEREDA: Yep...they're real people with real feelings too.

STARKISHA: What's gonna happen to our poor little Alicia?

ZEREDA: Who knows...but she'll be ok...she's tough.

STARLINDA: Are her and Cathy going to make it?

STARKSIHA: You know she's gonna be all messed up now and have intimacy issues.

(STARKISHA and STARLINDA exit.)

ZEREDA: Issues indeed. I think lesbians just have issues in general. They get married on the second date, have a puppy by the third, by the fourth they...well, let me just fast forward a bit for you. Two months later...

(CATHY enters.)

ALICIA: I'm so sorry I lied to my family! I promise I'll tell them. You're the only girl for me.

CATHY: Literally the only one...I was your first. Do you ever wish you had the chance to be with other girls?

ALICIA: No.

CATHY: I'm sorry you felt pressure.

ALICIA: I love you.

CATHY: I love you too.

ALICIA: Will you marry me?

CATHY: Oh, my God! Yes, of course.

ZEREDA: One month later...

CATHY: I am so tired of your Mexican Macho bullshit. You are turning out to be just like your mother!

ALICIA: You better be careful you don't turn out like your mother.

CATHY: I would love to be like my mother.

ALICIA: Well ya'll have one thing in common.

CATHY: What's that?

ALICIA: You both love sleeping with Mexicans.

CATHY: What are you talking about?

ALICIA: Don't act like you don't know. You mother is sleeping with Manuel her street pharmacist!

CATHY: How dare you talk about her like that?

ALICIA: Why the hell do you think she's always so happy? Ask her!

CATHY: Go to hell!

ALICIA: I was already there!

ZEREDA: Two weeks later...

CATHY: I'm so sorry.

ALICIA: No, I'm sorry.

CATHY/ALICIA: I love you.

ALICIA: I can't picture myself with anyone else.

CATHY: I want you to know that I do appreciate your culture. It's just different for me. Its uncomfortable when I'm the only white person in the room.

ALICIA: How do you think I feel every day at school?

CATHY: You could join the Spanish club?

ALICIA: I just feel like a sell out sometimes. I don't know what part of my home life to bring into my new life.

CATHY: Does your family even like white people?

ALICIA: Yes. What kind of question is that?

CATHY: Sometimes it seems like they just resent the fact that I'm white.

ALICIA: I can't change who my family is, all I can do is not allow them to change me.

ZEREDA: Three days later...

ALICIA: Get the fuck out!

(CATHY exits.STARKISHA, JOE and STARLINDA enter.)

ZEREDA: Maybe you should find yourself a nice Mexican girl?

ALICIA: You sound like my grandmother!

JOE: Have things gotten any better?

ALICIA: No. And they're making me drink some nasty tea three times a day...to cure me from the gay spirit...just in case, you know, just in case. Asshole. And my aunt was all wired that day!

JOE: At least they know you didn't choose this.

ALICIA: They'll always think it's my choice.

JOE: You can come live with me.

ALICIA: You're dirty.

JOE: Ungrateful bitch!

ZEREDA: You'll be fine. We'll be your family.ALICIA
I can't handle not having them.

ZEREDA: Then you shouldn't have come out.

JOE: I agree. If someone wouldn't have told my parents, then they'd never known.

ALICIA: But I didn't want to lose Cathy.

ZEREDA: She shouldn't have made you.

ALICIA: She didn't. It was my choice. You don't make it easier by talking bad about her. I love...loved her.

STARKISHA: Baby, that's what friends do...we talk shit.

STARLINDA: Then go get her back. If you really love her go get her!

ZEREDA: We promise we'll support you.

STARKISHA: Ok, we will. Baby, nobody really knows the truth behind a relationship besides the two people that are in it.

ALICIA: Thanks you guys. I better go. I have to drink my nasty tea before I drive back home.

JOE: It's not bad if you add sugar.

ZEREDA: I added rum to mine.

ALICIA: Thanks.

(ALICIA exits. STARKISHA and STARLINDA look at Zereda.)

STARKISHA: We're gonna follow her aren't we?

ZEREDA: Yup.

STARKISHA: I was afraid of that.

STARLINDA: So, drag mothers are kinda like stalkers?

ZEREDA: Yeah.

(THEY ALL exit.)

END OF SCENE

SCENE THREE

SETTING: KIKA's kitchen.

AT RISE: KIKA, MARIA and MAGUE are sitting at a table drinking coffee and cleaning beans.

MARIA: A que hora llega Alicia?

KIKA: Ya no tarda.

MAGUE: Is she coming home for good?

KIKA: No se.

MARIA: Que vas a ser si no se queda?

KIKA: No se.

MAGUE: Pues que sabes?

KIKA: MAGUE, por favor.

MAGUE: Nunca me acabaste te platicar que les paso a las brujas.

KIKA: La gente las corrió del pueblito.

MARIA: Cosas feas hicieron.

KIKA: Toda una generación de niños nacieron con susto porque sus mamas tenían miedo.

ALICIA: (Entering) I'm home.

    (MAGUE and MARIA get up and hug her.)

MAGUE: Hi, *mija*.

MARIA:How was your drive?

ALICIA: Good.

ALICIA: Ama. Como esta?

KIKA: Bien mija. Y tu?

ALICIA: Bien.

MAGUE: How long will you be here?

ALICIA: No se.

(A phone is hear. THEY ALL check their phones.)

ALICIA: It's mine.

KIKA: *Mija*, what's wrong?

ALICIA: It's my mom.

KIKA: How did she get your number?

ALICIA: I don't know.

KIKA: What does she want?

ALICIA: She wants to see if I'm ok.

KIKA: Ya pa'que.

MAGUE: How did she find out?

MARIA: I bet it was Maria Gomez.

KIKA: I'm sure. She's like a newspaper.

MARIA: She was sitting outside the confessional last time I went.

MAGUE: She does that all the time.

MARIA: And then she tells everyone on that Internet...you know where you can have a farm.

KIKA: How can you have a farm on the Internet?

MARIA: You can. You have to plant and water and harvest. If you don't *se te mueren las* plants. And sometimes you find lost cows.

KIKA: On the Internet?

MARIA: Yes!

ALICIA: She's talking about Facebook. Maria Gomez! That all makes sense now.

MAGUE: What makes sense?

ALICIA: She requested to be my friend and I added her cause all my other friends added her...I just figured she knew you guys. It turns out that all my friends added her cause we all thought one of us knew her.

KIKA: Enough about all this. What have you decided?

ALICIA: Well...

MARIA: Yes.

ALICIA: Well, I'm not with Cathy.

KIKA: Good.

ALICIA: That doesn't change the fact that I'm gay.

MARIA: No *mija*!

ALICIA: *Tía*, I can't help it.

MARIA: Then I can't help you. I can't turn my back on God.

(SHE exits.)

ALICIA: And you *Tia* MAGUE?

MAGUE: I don't know. I still love you *mija*.

ALICIA: I'm not asking that you like it or accept it. I just have to live my life.

MAGUE: I'll leave you two alone.

(SHE exits.)

ALICIA: Great. The one time I wish my nosey aunts would stick around.

KIKA: Are you hungry?

ALICIA: A little. Does this mean...

KIKA: I don't like it and I don't know that I will ever understand it but I love you and will try.

ALICIA: I promise I won't turn out like my mom.

KIKA: You could never be like your mom. I didn't kick her out cause she was gay. I kicked her out because she was not good to you. Promise me you'll finish school.

ALICIA: I promise.

KIKA: And you won't be a truck driver like everyone says.

ALICIA: I promise.

KIKA: And you won't bring home any more white girls.

(ALICIA just smiles.)

KIKA: Or Black girls.

ALICIA: I can't help who I fall in love with.

KIKA: Can you at least not fall in love with a *marijuana*?

ALICIA: I promise.

KIKA: And wear make-up?

ALICIA: Let's not push it.

KIKA: I made your favorite.

ALICIA: *Enchiladas* with an egg on top.

KIKA: How long are you staying?

ALICIA: I decided to come home for the summer to work.

KIKA: Good, *mija,* good.

ALICIA: *Ama*, do you have anything for a stomachache?

KIKA: I have *yerba buena* outside. I'll make you some tea.

END OF SCENE

SCENE FOUR

SETTING: A stage.

AT RISE: ZEREDA, STARKISHA, and STARLINDA are preparing their luggage.

STARLINDA: Where are we going now?

ZEREDA: Oklahoma.

STARLINDA: I didn't know they grew lesbians there.

STARKISHA: Uh-huh. Along with wheat, hay, and marijuana.

STARLINDA: At least we won't be bored.

ZEREDA: But first ladies...your crowns.

> (She takes two crowns out of a suitcase and places them on their heads.)

STARLINDA: But, is Alicia going to be OK? I don't know if we made things better or worse for her?

ZEREDA: Baby, queens always make things better.

STARKISHA: I know that's right. Damn lesbians be dressing like truck drivers if we weren't around.

STARLINDA: How comes you don't wear your crown?

ZEREDA: Baby, I don't need a crown to know I'm a queen...if you act like a queen you get treated like a queen. Now, hurry up ladies, we have to get ready for the drag show.

STARLINDA: I've been waiting for this moment since I was just a little boy in heels.

STARKISHA: Is saran wrap appropriate attire?

STARLINDA: *Cochina, te van a ver todo tu negocio.*

ZEREDA: See all you people at the club in a bit.

> (THEY exit. As they exit music begins to play and we transition into a club. ALICIA, MAGUE, KIKA, and MARIA enter the club.)

ALICIA: Hurry! Don't be scared. No one is gonna touch you. Maria, put the cross away! Come on!

KIKA: *Que es* un drag show?

> (MAGUE grabs a girl from the audience.)

MAGUE: What about this lesbian?

MARIA: She is kind of pretty. Is she Catholic? Are you Catholic? No, she doesn't look Catholic.

ALICIA: She's kinda hot.

MARIA: *No señorita!* She's not a good Catholic girl; lets go!

ALICIA: Call me!

KIKA: *Que es* un drag show!

MAGUE: I brought pictures.

MARIA/ALICIA: No!

MARIA: (To Alicia) *Alicia, mija...*I'm sorry.

ALICIA: It's ok.

(ZEREDA, STARKISHA, and STARLINDA begin to perform as the curtain closes.)

THE END

For all the little gay boys and girls...

www.ingramcontent.com/pod-product-compliance
Lightning Source LLC
Chambersburg PA
CBHW060411050426
42449CB00009B/1953